MONGOLIA
TRAVEL GUIDE 2023

Journey into Nomadic Culture:
Your Ultimate Mongolia Travel
Companion

Robben Charles

DISCLAIMER

The information provided in the "Mongolia Travel Guide 2023" by Robben Charles is intended for general informational purposes only. While every effort has been made to ensure the accuracy and currency of the content, the author and publisher do not guarantee its completeness or reliability.

Travel information, local conditions, and regulations can change rapidly, and readers are advised to independently verify any details before making travel plans. The author and publisher shall not be held liable for any inaccuracies, errors, or omissions in the content of this guide.

Travel involves inherent risks, and readers are encouraged to exercise caution and discretion while following the recommendations, advice, and suggestions provided in this guide. The author and publisher are not responsible for any accidents, injuries, losses, or damages that may occur as a result of using the information presented in this guide.

Readers should also be aware that cultural norms, local customs, and regulations in Mongolia may vary, and it is the responsibility of the traveler to be respectful and mindful of these differences. The author and publisher cannot be held responsible for any misunderstandings or cultural misinterpretations.

Furthermore, the mention of specific businesses, services, or establishments in this guide does not imply endorsement or recommendation by the author or publisher. Readers should conduct their own research and exercise their judgment when using any services or products mentioned.

By using this "Mongolia Travel Guide 2023," readers acknowledge and accept the limitations and disclaimers mentioned above. Travelers are advised to seek advice from official sources, local authorities, and qualified professionals when planning their trip to Mongolia.

TABLE OF CONTENTS

WELCOME TO MONGOLIA

Introduction to Mongolia

Geography and Climate

Mongolia, a landlocked country in East Asia, is known for its vast landscapes, rich cultural heritage, and unique nomadic traditions. Covering an area of over 1.5 million square kilometers, Mongolia is one of the world's least densely populated countries. Its geography is characterized by diverse features, from expansive steppes to rugged mountains and sprawling deserts.

Geography:

Mongolia is situated between Russia to the north and China to the south, with a small section bordering Kazakhstan in the west. The country is divided into several geographical regions. The vast grasslands, known as steppes, dominate the central and eastern parts of the country, providing grazing areas for Mongolia's famous nomadic herders. The northern region is home to the Khövsgöl Lake, one of the world's largest freshwater lakes by volume. To the south lies the

Gobi Desert, a vast and arid expanse known for its unique ecosystem and harsh conditions.

Climate:

Mongolia experiences a continental climate with distinct seasons. Summers (June to August) are warm, with temperatures often exceeding 30°C (86°F) in some regions. Winters (December to February) are extremely cold, with temperatures dropping well below freezing, especially in the northern and central areas. The Gobi Desert can experience dramatic temperature variations, with scorching daytime highs and chilly nights. Spring and autumn are relatively short but pleasant transitional periods.

Travel Considerations:

When planning a trip to Mongolia, it's essential to pack for varying weather conditions, as the climate can change drastically. Summer is the most popular time for tourism, offering milder temperatures and easier travel conditions. Winter attracts adventure enthusiasts looking to experience the country's unique ice festivals and winter sports.

Understanding Mongolia's geography and climate will help travelers make the most of their visit, whether exploring the ancient capital of Ulaanbaatar, witnessing traditional festivals, or embarking on nomadic adventures across the stunning landscapes.

Cultural Diversity

Mongolia's cultural tapestry is woven from a rich blend of history, tradition, and nomadic heritage. As a country that has been influenced by neighboring nations while maintaining its distinct identity, Mongolia offers travelers a unique and captivating cultural experience.

Nomadic Heritage:
Nomadic life is deeply ingrained in Mongolia's culture. The vast grasslands, or steppes, have historically supported the nomadic way of life, where herding livestock like horses, yaks, and camels has been central to survival. Traditional gers (yurts), portable round tents, are symbolic of this lifestyle, providing shelter that can be easily moved with the herds.

Language and Religion:
The official language of Mongolia is Mongolian, written in the Cyrillic script. Mongolian culture has strong ties to Tibetan Buddhism, with many monasteries and temples across the country. The most famous is the Gandantegchinlen Monastery

in Ulaanbaatar, known for its impressive statue of Megjid Janraisig (Avalokiteshvara), the Buddhist deity of compassion.

Festivals and Celebrations:
Mongolia's festivals offer a glimpse into its vibrant traditions. The Naadam Festival, celebrated in July, is a major highlight featuring traditional sports like wrestling, archery, and horse racing. Tsagaan Sar, the Lunar New Year, is a significant event where families gather to welcome the coming year with feasting and gift-giving.

Music and Arts:
Mongolian music is characterized by its distinctive throat-singing or "khöömii," a technique that produces multiple notes simultaneously. Traditional instruments like the morin khuur (horsehead fiddle) and yatga (zither) are integral to Mongolian music. The arts often depict nomadic life, nature, and historical events.

Hospitality and Etiquette:
Mongolians are known for their warm hospitality and respect for guests. When visiting a ger, it's

customary to offer a simple bow upon entering and avoid stepping on the threshold. Offering traditional dairy products like airag (fermented mare's milk) is a sign of goodwill.

Exploring Mongolia's cultural diversity allows travelers to connect with its unique history and heritage. From participating in traditional activities to engaging with local communities, visitors can gain a deeper understanding of the country's rich cultural tapestry.

History and Heritage

Mongolia's history stretches back thousands of years, marked by the rise and fall of empires, legendary conquerors, and a deep connection to nomadic traditions. This storied past has left an indelible mark on the country's heritage, making it a captivating destination for travelers seeking insight into its historical evolution.

Early History:
Mongolia's history can be traced back to ancient times, with early inhabitants engaged in hunting, gathering, and eventually domesticating animals for sustenance. The Xiongnu and Hunnic confederations are among the earliest known societies to have occupied the region, followed by the Turkic Khaganate and the Uighur Empire.

Mongol Empire:
The most well-known chapter in Mongolia's history is the rise of Genghis Khan and the establishment of the Mongol Empire in the 13th century. Under Genghis Khan's leadership, the empire expanded to become the largest contiguous

land empire in history, spanning from Asia to Europe. The empire's influence on global trade, culture, and diplomacy was immense.

Nomadic Traditions:
The Mongol Empire's legacy also extends to the preservation of nomadic traditions. While the empire dissolved, the nomadic way of life persisted, with various clans and tribes wandering the vast steppes. This lifestyle fostered a unique cultural identity centered around horsemanship, herding, and the use of portable gers (yurts) as dwellings.

Chinese Influence and Independence:
In subsequent centuries, Mongolia came under Chinese rule during the Qing Dynasty. However, Mongolia's aspiration for independence remained steadfast. The early 20th century witnessed a series of events that eventually led to Mongolia gaining its independence from China in 1921, with support from the Soviet Red Army.

Modern Mongolia:

The 20th century also brought significant changes to Mongolia, including periods of Soviet influence during the Cold War era. In 1990, Mongolia transitioned to a democratic system, marking a turning point in its modern history. Today, the country balances its rich heritage with a growing modernization drive.

Heritage and Landmarks:
Mongolia's historical heritage is preserved in its ancient monasteries, archaeological sites, and artifacts. The Erdene Zuu Monastery, dating back to the 16th century, is one of the oldest and most important Buddhist monasteries in Mongolia. The ancient capital city of Karakorum, established by Genghis Khan, holds remnants of the empire's grandeur.

Exploring Mongolia's history and heritage provides travelers with a deeper appreciation for the country's resilience, cultural continuity, and its role in shaping the world's historical narrative. From the legacy of Genghis Khan to the enduring nomadic lifestyle, visitors can uncover the layers of history that have shaped modern-day Mongolia.

Planning Your Trip

Visa and Entry Requirements

Visa and Entry Requirements for Mongolia:
As of my last update in September 2021, the visa and entry requirements for Mongolia could have changed. It's important to double-check with the official authorities or the Mongolian embassy in your country for the most up-to-date information. However, here's a general overview:

1. Visa-Free Travel: Some nationalities are allowed to enter Mongolia visa-free for certain periods. For example, citizens of Japan, Malaysia, Singapore, the United States, and many European countries can enter Mongolia without a visa for stays of up to 30 days for tourism purposes. However, the exact duration and conditions may vary, so check with the Mongolian embassy.

2. Visa-On-Arrival: Some nationalities can obtain a visa on arrival at the Chinggis Khaan International Airport in Ulaanbaatar. This option might allow you to stay for up to 30 days. Again, this information might have changed, so verify before you travel.

3. Tourist Visa: If you're not eligible for visa-free travel or visa on arrival, you'll likely need to apply for a tourist visa in advance. This usually involves submitting an application, a passport-sized photo, a valid passport, and potentially other documents like a travel itinerary and proof of accommodations.

4. Invitation Letter: Sometimes, you might need an invitation letter from a Mongolian travel agency or an individual living in Mongolia to support your visa application. Check the specific requirements for your nationality.

5. Duration Extensions: If you wish to stay in Mongolia for longer than the allowed visa-free period or the duration of your visa, you can apply for an extension through the Immigration Agency of Mongolia.

6. Transit: If you're transiting through Mongolia to another destination and won't leave the airport, you may not need a visa. However, confirm this with the relevant authorities.

Always ensure you have a valid passport with at least six months' validity beyond your intended departure date. Additionally, regulations can change, so it's wise to consult official sources or the Mongolian embassy in your country before making travel arrangements.

Remember, entry requirements can change, and it's important to stay updated with the latest information from official sources before you travel.

Best Time to Visit

Best Time to Visit Mongolia:

Mongolia offers a unique travel experience with its vast landscapes, rich culture, and diverse weather patterns. The best time to visit depends on your preferences and the type of activities you want to engage in.

1. Summer (June to August):

The summer months are the most popular time to visit Mongolia. During this period, the weather is relatively warm, with temperatures ranging from 15°C to 25°C (59°F to 77°F) in most regions. The countryside comes alive with lush greenery and colorful wildflowers, making it an ideal time for outdoor activities such as trekking, horseback riding, and camping. The famous Naadam Festival, featuring traditional Mongolian sports like wrestling, archery, and horse racing, usually takes place in July.

2. Fall (September to October):

Fall is another excellent time to visit Mongolia. The weather starts to cool down, but the landscapes are still vibrant with autumn foliage. September offers pleasant temperatures, ranging from 10°C to 20°C (50°F to 68°F), making it a good time for trekking and cultural exploration. This is also the time when the Gobi Desert is more accessible and comfortable to explore.

3. Winter (November to February):

Winter in Mongolia is known for its extreme cold, with temperatures plummeting to as low as -40°C (-40°F) in some areas. However, if you're interested in experiencing the unique winter culture of Mongolia, this could be an adventurous time to visit. The Winter Festival, held in February, showcases traditional winter sports, ice sculpture contests, and camel and horse racing on frozen lakes.

4. Spring (March to May):

Spring in Mongolia is a transition period characterized by fluctuating temperatures. It's a good time to witness the reawakening of nature as the snow melts and the landscapes start to turn green. However, the weather can still be chilly, and many roads might not be accessible due to the melting snow.

Travel Considerations:

When planning your trip to Mongolia, consider the following:

- **Weather Preparation:** The weather can be unpredictable, so pack accordingly. Layered clothing and gear suitable for various weather conditions are essential.
- **Altitude:** Mongolia has varying elevations, so if you plan to visit high-altitude areas, be mindful of altitude sickness.
- **Accommodation:** Accommodations may be limited in remote areas, so make reservations in advance, especially during peak tourist seasons.
- **Local Customs:** Familiarize yourself with Mongolian customs and traditions to ensure respectful interactions with locals.
- **Travel Restrictions:** Keep an eye on travel advisories and restrictions, especially considering the global situation in 2023.

Ultimately, the best time to visit Mongolia depends on your interests, whether you want to experience its festivals, explore the outdoors, or witness the distinct beauty of its changing seasons.

Travel Budgeting

Travel Budgeting for Mongolia:

Budgeting for a trip to Mongolia involves considering various factors, such as accommodation, transportation, food, activities, and unexpected expenses. Keep in mind that costs can vary based on your travel style, preferences, and the duration of your stay.

1. Accommodation:

Accommodation costs in Mongolia can range from budget-friendly guesthouses and hostels to luxury hotels. In major cities like Ulaanbaatar, you'll find a variety of options. Outside the cities, ger camps (traditional felt tents) are a unique and popular choice. Prices for accommodations can vary widely, but budget travelers can expect to pay around $20 to $50 per night for mid-range options.

2. Transportation:

Transportation costs will depend on how you plan to get around. Internal flights, if necessary, can add to your budget. The most common mode of transportation is by road, using buses, shared vans, or renting a vehicle. Train journeys are also an option, offering scenic routes between Ulaanbaatar and some other cities. Budget around $10 to $30 per day for local transportation.

3. Food:

Eating out in Mongolia is relatively affordable, especially if you stick to local eateries and markets. Traditional Mongolian dishes like buuz (dumplings) and khuushuur (fried pastries) are budget-friendly options. A meal at a mid-range restaurant might cost around $10 to $20, while street food and local markets can offer even more economical choices.

4. Activities and Sightseeing:

The cost of activities will depend on what you want to do. Entry fees for attractions, guided tours, and outdoor activities like horseback riding and trekking will be additional expenses. Plan your activities in advance to estimate costs accurately.

5. Miscellaneous Expenses:

Factor in additional expenses like visa fees (if applicable), travel insurance, souvenirs, and any unforeseen costs. It's wise to have a buffer of around 10-20% of your total budget for unexpected expenses.

6. Sample Budget:
For a budget traveler, a daily budget of $40 to $60 can provide a comfortable experience, covering mid-range accommodation, local transportation, meals, and basic activities. Mid-range travelers might expect to spend around $70 to $120 per day, while luxury travelers should budget higher.

Remember that these estimates are approximate and can vary based on personal preferences and circumstances. Research and plan ahead to get a clearer picture of the costs you can expect for your specific travel style and itinerary. It's also advisable to have a mix of local currency (Mongolian Tugrik) and a credit card for convenience and security.

Packing Essentials

Packing Essentials for Mongolia:

Packing for Mongolia requires careful consideration of the diverse weather conditions and the activities you plan to engage in. Whether you're exploring the Gobi Desert or enjoying the cultural attractions in Ulaanbaatar, having the right essentials will enhance your travel experience.

1. Clothing:

- **Layering is Key:** Mongolia experiences fluctuating temperatures, so pack clothes that can be layered. This includes lightweight base layers, warm sweaters, and a waterproof outer layer.
- **Warm Clothing:** Even during the summer months, nights and early mornings can be chilly. Bring a warm jacket or fleece for those cooler moments.
- **Sturdy Footwear:** Comfortable hiking boots or sturdy walking shoes are essential for outdoor activities and exploring uneven terrain.
- **Rain Gear:** A waterproof jacket and pants will keep you dry during sudden rain showers.

- **Headgear:** A hat or cap to shield you from the sun and keep you warm in colder weather.
- **Gloves and Scarf:** These will be handy during cooler months or if you're planning to spend time in higher altitudes.

2. Outdoor Gear:
- **Backpack:** A durable backpack is essential for carrying your essentials during day trips and outdoor adventures.
- **Sleeping Bag:** If you plan to stay in ger camps or go camping, a suitable sleeping bag is a must.

3. Travel Accessories:
- **Sun Protection:** Sunscreen, sunglasses, and a wide-brimmed hat to protect against the strong Mongolian sun.
- **Insect Repellent:** Depending on your itinerary, insect repellent might be necessary.
- **Reusable Water Bottle:** Staying hydrated is important, especially in the dry climate. A reusable water bottle with a filter is convenient and eco-friendly.

- **Universal Power Adapter:** Mongolia uses Type C and E sockets, so a universal adapter will be handy for charging your devices.
- **First Aid Kit:** Include essentials like adhesive bandages, antiseptic wipes, pain relievers, and any necessary prescription medications.

4. Personal Items:

- **Passport and Copies:** Always carry your passport and keep photocopies or digital copies in a separate place.
- **Travel Insurance:** Make sure you have comprehensive travel insurance that covers medical emergencies and other unforeseen situations.
- **Cash and Cards:** Carry some local currency (Mongolian Tugrik) for smaller purchases, and have a credit card as a backup.
- **Electronics:** Phone, camera, chargers, and any other devices you might need. A portable power bank can be useful.

5. Cultural Considerations:

- **Respectful Attire:** If you plan to visit monasteries or more conservative areas, consider packing clothing that covers your shoulders and knees as a sign of respect.

6. Miscellaneous:
- **Language Guide:** A pocket-sized Mongolian phrasebook can be helpful for communication.
- **Map or Navigation App:** A physical map or offline navigation app will come in handy, especially in remote areas.

Remember that the key is to pack efficiently while keeping your comfort and the activities you plan to do in mind. Mongolia's landscapes and weather can vary greatly, so being prepared will enhance your travel experience.

Getting to Mongolia

International Airports

Mongolia has three main international airports that cater to travelers:

1. Chinggis Khaan International Airport (ULN): Located in the capital city, Ulaanbaatar, this is the primary gateway to Mongolia. It offers connections to various international destinations, including China, Russia, South Korea, and Turkey. The airport has modern facilities, including duty-free shops, currency exchange services, and restaurants.

2. Buyant Ukhaa International Airport (UGT): Also situated in Ulaanbaatar, this airport mainly handles domestic flights but has limited international connections. It's a convenient option if you're looking to explore other parts of Mongolia.

3. Altai Airport (LTI): Located in the western province of Bayan-Ölgii, Altai Airport serves as a connection to neighboring countries like Kazakhstan. It's particularly useful if you're planning to explore the Altai Mountains and the Kazakh culture in the region.

Keep in mind that flight availability and routes can vary seasonally, so it's a good idea to check with airlines for the most up-to-date information when planning your trip.

Land Border Crossings

Mongolia shares its borders with two countries, Russia to the north and China to the south. There are several land border crossings that travelers can use to enter Mongolia:

1. **Zamyn-Üüd / Erlian:** This is one of the main border crossings between Mongolia and China. On the Mongolian side, it's known as Zamyn-Üüd, and on the Chinese side, it's called Erlian. This crossing is popular among travelers coming from Beijing or exploring the Trans-Siberian Railway, as it offers a direct route to Ulaanbaatar.

2. **Altanbulag / Kyakhta:** This crossing connects Mongolia with Russia. On the Mongolian side, it's Altanbulag, and on the Russian side, it's Kyakhta. It's commonly used by travelers on the Trans-Siberian Railway or those exploring the Lake Baikal region.

3. **Tsagaannuur / Tashanta:** Located in the far western part of Mongolia, this crossing connects with Russia's Tuva Republic. It's less frequented by

tourists but offers access to the stunning landscapes of western Mongolia.

4. Bichigt / Muren: This border crossing links Mongolia with Russia's Buryat Republic. It's a quieter crossing and may be more suitable for travelers looking for a less crowded route.

5. Gashuunsukhait / Gants Mod: Situated in the southern part of Mongolia, this crossing connects with China. On the Mongolian side, it's called Gashuunsukhait, and on the Chinese side, it's Gants Mod. This route provides access to the Gobi Desert and southern regions of Mongolia.

When using land border crossings, it's important to check the current visa requirements and regulations for both Mongolia and the neighboring country you're entering from. Keep in mind that border crossing procedures can vary, and it's a good idea to plan ahead and have all necessary documents in order.

Transportation within the Country

1. Domestic Flights:

Mongolia has a few domestic airports that connect major cities and regional centers. These flights are especially useful for covering long distances quickly, such as between Ulaanbaatar and destinations like Khovd, Ölgii, or Dalanzadgad. Keep in mind that flight schedules might change due to weather conditions, so it's advisable to confirm your flights in advance.

2. Train Travel:

Mongolia's train system is centered around the Trans-Mongolian Railway, which connects Moscow in Russia to Beijing in China. This route passes through Ulaanbaatar, offering a unique and scenic way to explore the country. Trains have varying levels of comfort, from standard compartments to more luxurious options, depending on your preference.

3. Buses and Minivans:

Buses and minivans (known as "microbuses") are common for travel within cities and between towns. They are generally affordable and frequent, though comfort levels can vary. Buses are a popular option for shorter distances, while microbuses often serve smaller routes or areas not covered by larger buses.

4. Shared Taxis and Hitchhiking:
In rural areas, shared taxis are a common mode of transportation. These are usually cars that operate on fixed routes, picking up and dropping off passengers along the way. Hitchhiking is also relatively common, especially in remote regions where public transportation might be limited.

5. Renting a Vehicle:
For travelers seeking more independence, renting a car or a 4x4 vehicle is an option. This allows you to explore Mongolia's vast landscapes at your own pace. However, keep in mind that roads outside major cities can be challenging, and having some off-road driving experience is beneficial.

6. Horseback Riding:

Horseback riding is a traditional and unique way to travel in Mongolia, especially in rural areas. Many nomadic families offer horse treks for tourists, allowing you to experience the country's cultural heritage while enjoying its stunning scenery.

7. Camels and Bactrian Camels:
In certain regions, such as the Gobi Desert, camels and Bactrian camels (with two humps) are used for transportation. These animals are well-suited to the desert terrain and offer a different way to explore remote areas.

As you plan your travels within Mongolia, it's important to be flexible and prepare for possible delays, especially in more remote areas. Researching your chosen mode of transportation and routes beforehand will help you make the most of your journey.

Exploring Ulaanbaatar

Top Attractions

Ulaanbaatar Overview:
Ulaanbaatar, the capital city of Mongolia, offers a unique blend of modern development and rich cultural heritage. As the country's largest city, it serves as a gateway to the vast landscapes and nomadic culture of Mongolia.

Top Attractions:

1. **Sükhbaatar Square:** The central square is named after Damdin Sükhbaatar, a national hero of Mongolia. It's a historical and political hub, surrounded by important buildings like the Government Palace and the Mongolian Stock Exchange.

2. **Gandan Monastery:** This Buddhist monastery is home to the country's largest standing statue of Buddha, and it offers a glimpse into Mongolia's

spiritual side. Visitors can witness monks engaged in prayers and rituals.

3. National Museum of Mongolia: Here, you can explore the country's history, culture, and heritage. The museum's exhibits cover topics ranging from prehistoric times to the modern era, including traditional costumes, artifacts, and historical documents.

4. Choijin Lama Temple Museum: A preserved 19th-century monastery, this museum showcases exquisite artwork, sculptures, and religious relics. It provides insight into Mongolia's religious history and artistic craftsmanship.

5. Zaisan Memorial: For panoramic views of the city, head to Zaisan Memorial, a hilltop monument dedicated to Soviet-Mongolian friendship. The surrounding area offers great photo opportunities.

6. Winter Palace of the Bogd Khan: This palace was the residence of Mongolia's last king and is now a museum displaying his personal belongings, art, and artifacts. The surrounding gardens add to the charm of the place.

7. Bogd Khan Uul National Park: Just south of the city, this national park offers hiking trails, beautiful scenery, and the chance to spot wildlife. It's a perfect escape for nature enthusiasts.

8. Naran Tuul Market (Black Market): A vibrant market where you can find traditional Mongolian clothing, souvenirs, antiques, and various goods. It's a great place to experience local shopping culture.

Travel Tips:

- **Weather:** Ulaanbaatar experiences extreme temperatures, so pack accordingly for both cold winters and warm summers.

- **Transport:** Getting around the city is convenient with taxis and buses. However, be prepared for traffic congestion during peak hours.

- **Cuisine:** Try traditional Mongolian dishes such as khorkhog (slow-cooked meat and vegetables), buuz (steamed dumplings), and airag (fermented mare's milk).

- **Cultural Etiquette:** Mongolian culture places a strong emphasis on hospitality and respect. It's polite to offer and receive items with your right hand, and when visiting a ger (traditional tent), it's customary to enter with your right foot first.

Remember that Mongolia offers much more beyond Ulaanbaatar, with vast steppes, desert landscapes, and nomadic traditions waiting to be explored. Enjoy your journey!

Accommodation Options

Accommodation Options:

1. Hotels: Ulaanbaatar offers a range of hotels catering to various budgets and preferences. From luxury international chains to boutique hotels and budget options, you'll find a variety of choices. Some well-known hotels include the Shangri-La, Kempinski, and Ramada.

2. Guesthouses: Guesthouses provide a more intimate and local experience. They are often family-run and offer a chance to interact with locals. This option is particularly popular among budget travelers and those looking for a more authentic stay.

3. Hostels: Hostels are a great choice for solo travelers or those looking to meet fellow travelers. They offer affordable dormitory-style accommodation as well as private rooms. Some hostels also organize tours and activities.

4. Ger Camps: For a unique experience, consider staying in a traditional Mongolian ger (yurt). While these are more common in the countryside, there are ger camps on the outskirts of Ulaanbaatar where you can enjoy the nomadic lifestyle.

5. Serviced Apartments: If you're planning an extended stay or prefer more space and privacy, serviced apartments are available. These come with kitchen facilities and are suitable for families or those on business trips.

6. Airbnb: There are Airbnb listings available in Ulaanbaatar, offering a variety of accommodations ranging from private apartments to traditional gers.

Choosing Accommodation:

- **Location:** Consider staying near major attractions or transportation hubs for convenience. The Sukhbaatar Square area and Peace Avenue are popular central locations.

- **Amenities:** Check for amenities that matter to you, such as Wi-Fi, breakfast, fitness facilities, and airport shuttle services.

- **Reviews:** Read guest reviews to get an idea of the quality of service, cleanliness, and overall guest experience.

- **Price Range:** Ulaanbaatar offers accommodation options for various budgets. Keep in mind that prices can vary based on the season and local events.

Booking Tips:

- **Advance Booking:** During peak tourist seasons, it's advisable to book accommodation in advance to secure your preferred option.

- **Online Platforms:** Use booking websites and apps to compare prices, read reviews, and make reservations.

- **Local Advice:** Seek advice from fellow travelers or locals for recommendations on hidden gems and unique places to stay.

Remember that Ulaanbaatar's accommodation options may differ from standard Western offerings, especially if you opt for guesthouses or traditional gers. Plan ahead, choose according to your preferences, and enjoy your stay in this fascinating city!

Dining and Nightlife

Dining Options:

1. Traditional Mongolian Cuisine: Don't miss the opportunity to try authentic Mongolian dishes. Sample dishes like khorkhog (slow-cooked meat and vegetables), buuz (steamed dumplings), and khuushuur (fried meat pies) at local restaurants and eateries.

2. International Cuisine: Ulaanbaatar boasts a diverse culinary scene. You'll find restaurants offering cuisines from around the world, including Korean, Japanese, Chinese, Italian, and more.

3. Local Markets and Street Food: Explore local markets like Naran Tuul Market (Black Market) for a taste of Mongolian street food. Look for grilled meat skewers, fried pastries, and dairy products like aaruul (dried curd).

4. Fine Dining: For an upscale dining experience, there are fine dining restaurants in the city offering gourmet cuisine and exquisite settings.

5. Cafés and Bakeries: Ulaanbaatar has a growing café culture. Enjoy freshly brewed coffee, pastries, and light meals at various cafés and bakeries.

Nightlife Options:

1. Bars and Pubs: Ulaanbaatar has a vibrant nightlife scene with numerous bars and pubs. Enjoy local beers, cocktails, and a mix of live music and DJs.

2. Clubs: If you're looking to dance the night away, there are several clubs that play a mix of international and local music. Some clubs also host theme nights and special events.

3. Live Music Venues: Experience live music performances, including traditional Mongolian music and contemporary genres, at various venues around the city.

4. Cultural Performances: Check if there are any cultural performances or shows happening during your visit. These might include traditional throat singing, contortionist acts, and folk dances.

Nightlife Tips:

- **Opening Hours:** Nightlife venues in Ulaanbaatar often stay open late, especially on weekends. Many establishments open around 9 or 10 PM and continue until the early hours of the morning.

- **Safety:** While Ulaanbaatar is generally safe, it's advisable to take common-sense precautions, such as not leaving drinks unattended and being cautious when exploring unfamiliar areas at night.

- **Local Recommendations:** To discover the best spots for dining and nightlife, ask locals or fellow travelers for recommendations.

- **Dress Code:** Some upscale venues might have a dress code, so it's a good idea to inquire in advance.

Remember that Ulaanbaatar's dining and nightlife scene continues to evolve, so staying updated on the latest trends and popular spots can enhance your experience of the city's culture and entertainment.

Outdoor Adventures

The Gobi Desert

Introduction:

Mongolia's Gobi Desert is a captivating destination for outdoor enthusiasts and adventure seekers alike. Stretching across southern Mongolia, this vast and diverse landscape offers a unique blend of natural wonders, cultural experiences, and adrenaline-pumping activities. In this travel guide, we'll delve into the must-see attractions, thrilling activities, and essential tips for making the most of your Gobi Desert adventure in 2023.

Must-See Attractions:

1. Flaming Cliffs (Bayanzag): Known for its stunning red rock formations and being a hotspot for dinosaur fossils, the Flaming Cliffs provide an otherworldly backdrop for exploration.

2. Khongoryn Els Sand Dunes: Often referred to as the "Singing Sands," these towering dunes offer breathtaking sunrise and sunset views. Adventure seekers can try sandboarding or camel trekking.

3. Yolyn Am Canyon: Nestled within the Gobi Gurvansaikhan National Park, this narrow gorge features ice formations even during the summer months. It's an excellent spot for hiking and birdwatching.

4. Ongi Monastery Ruins: Explore the remnants of a historic monastery complex that once stood along the banks of the Ongi River. The site provides a glimpse into Mongolia's rich cultural heritage.

Thrilling Activities:

1. Camel Trekking: Embark on a camel trek across the desert, following ancient caravan routes. This immersive experience allows you to connect with the nomadic way of life and take in the vastness of the Gobi.

2. Hiking and Trekking: The Gobi Desert offers various hiking and trekking trails, catering to different skill levels. From gentle walks to challenging hikes, there's something for everyone.

3. Stargazing: With minimal light pollution, the Gobi Desert is a paradise for stargazers. Marvel at the clear night skies and constellations that appear vividly in this remote location.

4. Photography Expeditions: Capture the stark beauty of the Gobi through your lens. The diverse landscapes, unique flora, and fauna make for exceptional photography opportunities.

Essential Tips:

1. Pack Wisely: Due to fluctuating temperatures, pack layers and clothing suitable for both hot days and cool nights. Don't forget sun protection and sturdy footwear.

2. Stay Hydrated: The desert's dry climate requires constant hydration. Carry an ample supply of water and replenish regularly.

3. Respect Local Customs: If interacting with nomadic families, show respect for their way of life and follow their customs. Always ask for permission before taking photos.

4. Travel with a Guide: Given the remote nature of the Gobi Desert, traveling with a knowledgeable local guide is highly recommended. They can enhance your experience, ensure your safety, and provide insights into the region's history and culture.

Conclusion:

Mongolia's Gobi Desert beckons adventurous souls with its unparalleled natural beauty and outdoor activities. From the enchanting Flaming Cliffs to the mesmerizing sand dunes, the Gobi offers a journey filled with awe-inspiring sights and unforgettable experiences. By following these tips and recommendations, you're well-equipped to embark on a memorable adventure through one of the world's most captivating desert landscapes.

Khuvsgul Lake and Northern Mongolia

Introduction:

For travelers seeking untouched wilderness and pristine landscapes, Khuvsgul Lake and the northern region of Mongolia offer an unrivaled outdoor adventure. Nestled within the vast Siberian taiga, this area boasts crystal-clear lakes, dense forests, and unique cultural experiences. In this travel guide, we'll explore the must-visit attractions, exhilarating activities, and practical tips for an unforgettable journey through Khuvsgul Lake and northern Mongolia in 2023.

Must-Visit Attractions:

1. Khuvsgul Lake: Often referred to as the "Blue Pearl of Mongolia," Khuvsgul Lake is one of the largest freshwater lakes in the country. Its stunning azure waters are surrounded by picturesque mountains and lush forests.

2. Reindeer Herders: Immerse yourself in the traditional lifestyle of the Dukha (Tsaatan) people, who rely on reindeer herding. Visit their remote camps and learn about their unique culture and customs.

3. **Tsaatan Nuur (Reindeer Lake):** Journey through dense forests to reach this remote and pristine alpine lake, where you can witness the Dukha people and their reindeer herds.

4. **Khoridol Saridag Mountains:** Embark on a trek through this range, home to diverse wildlife and rare plants. The stunning landscapes provide excellent opportunities for hiking and photography.

Exhilarating Activities:

1. **Horse Trekking:** Explore the stunning scenery on horseback, following ancient trails that wind through forests, valleys, and along the shores of Khuvsgul Lake.

2. **Boating and Fishing:** Experience the tranquility of Khuvsgul Lake by renting a traditional Mongolian boat. Fishing enthusiasts can try their luck at catching Arctic grayling and lenok trout.

3. Hiking and Camping: The region offers various hiking trails suitable for different skill levels. Camp by the lake's shores or in the wilderness for an immersive experience.

4. Cultural Immersion: Interact with the local Dukha people to learn about their unique way of life. Participate in activities like milking reindeer and crafting traditional items.

Practical Tips:

1. Weather Preparation: The northern region's weather can be unpredictable. Pack warm clothing, rain gear, and layers to adapt to changing conditions.

2. Responsible Tourism: Show respect for the environment and local communities. Follow Leave No Trace principles and be mindful of cultural sensitivities.

3. Language Considerations: English may not be widely spoken in remote areas. Consider learning a few basic Mongolian phrases or hiring a local guide for smooth communication.

4. Permit Requirements: Some areas, especially near the Russian border, might require special permits. Check with local authorities or your tour operator for up-to-date information.

Conclusion:

Khuvsgul Lake and northern Mongolia offer an unparalleled opportunity to connect with nature, experience unique cultures, and embark on thrilling outdoor adventures. From the turquoise waters of Khuvsgul Lake to the traditional lifestyle of the Dukha people, this region beckons travelers seeking a genuine and transformative journey. By embracing the activities and tips outlined in this guide, you'll be well-prepared to create lasting memories in one of Mongolia's most captivating and untouched landscapes.

Terelj National Park

Introduction:

Nestled within the rugged landscapes of Mongolia, Terelj National Park stands as a haven for outdoor enthusiasts seeking a blend of natural beauty and exhilarating activities. Just a stone's throw away from the capital city, Ulaanbaatar, this park offers a diverse range of experiences, from breathtaking rock formations to nomadic culture. In this travel guide, we'll dive into the must-see attractions, thrilling activities, and essential tips for a memorable adventure in Terelj National Park in 2023.

Must-See Attractions:

1. Turtle Rock (Melkhii Khad): A unique rock formation that resembles a turtle, this landmark is a symbol of Terelj National Park and a popular spot for photos.

2. Aryabal Meditation Temple: Perched atop a hill, this temple offers panoramic views of the park and is a serene spot for reflection and meditation.

3. Tuvkhun Monastery: Hidden in the mountains, this historic monastery provides insight into Mongolia's Buddhist heritage. A hike to the monastery offers both cultural and natural exploration.

4. Gorkhi-Terelj National Park: Beyond the famous landmarks, explore the park's diverse ecosystems, including forests, meadows, and rivers, which are home to various wildlife species.

Exhilarating Activities:
1. Hiking and Trekking: Terelj National Park offers a plethora of hiking trails, catering to different fitness levels. Explore the park's beauty on foot, from easy walks to challenging treks.

2. Rock Climbing: The unique rock formations in the park attract rock climbers of all skill levels. Whether you're a beginner or an experienced climber, there are routes to challenge and thrill you.

3. Horseback Riding: Embrace Mongolia's nomadic culture by embarking on a horseback adventure through the park's vast landscapes. It's a fantastic way to immerse yourself in the local way of life.

4. Yurt Stays: Experience authentic Mongolian hospitality by staying in a traditional yurt (ger). This unique accommodation option allows you to connect with nature while enjoying comfort.

Essential Tips:

1. Weather Preparedness: Mongolia's weather can be unpredictable. Pack layers, warm clothing, and rain gear to stay comfortable in changing conditions.

2. Respectful Interaction: If you encounter nomadic families, show respect for their way of life and ask for permission before taking photos. Engaging with locals can provide rich cultural insights.

3. Travel Season: The best time to visit Terelj National Park is during the warmer months, from May to September, when the weather is more favorable for outdoor activities.

4. Local Cuisine: Taste traditional Mongolian dishes such as khorkhog (meat stew), buuz (dumplings), and airag (fermented mare's milk) for a complete cultural experience.

Conclusion:
Terelj National Park offers an enticing blend of natural beauty, adventurous activities, and cultural immersion that makes it an ideal destination for outdoor enthusiasts and explorers. From awe-inspiring rock formations to the tranquil atmosphere of a yurt stay, the park's offerings are as diverse as they are captivating. By following the tips and embracing the experiences detailed in this guide, you'll be well-prepared to create lasting memories and embark on a remarkable journey through the breathtaking landscapes of Terelj National Park in 2023.

Horseback Riding and Nomadic Culture

Introduction:

Mongolia's vast landscapes and rich nomadic heritage offer a unique opportunity for travelers to engage in outdoor adventures while immersing themselves in the authentic lifestyle of the local nomadic communities. Horseback riding serves as both a mode of exploration and a connection to the country's traditional way of life. In this travel guide, we'll delve into the captivating world of horseback riding and nomadic culture, highlighting the must-try experiences and essential tips for an unforgettable journey in 2023.

Exploring Mongolia on Horseback:

1. Connection with Nature: Horseback riding allows you to traverse Mongolia's expansive terrains, from rolling grasslands to rugged mountains, offering an intimate connection with the country's diverse ecosystems.

2. Cultural Significance: Horses are an integral part of Mongolian culture, symbolizing freedom and resilience. Riding horses as the locals do provides a genuine insight into their way of life.

3. Adventurous Expeditions: Embark on multi-day horse treks across the steppe, following ancient nomadic routes. Experience the thrill of camping under the starlit skies and waking up to breathtaking vistas.

4. Flexible Riding Levels: Whether you're an experienced rider or a beginner, Mongolia offers horseback experiences tailored to your skill level, making it accessible for everyone.

Nomadic Culture Immersion:
1. Stay in Ger Camps: Experience the authentic nomadic lifestyle by staying in traditional felt-covered gers (yurts). These camps provide a comfortable base while allowing you to engage with local families.

2. Participate in Daily Activities: Join nomadic families in their daily chores, such as herding livestock, milking animals, and preparing traditional meals. This hands-on engagement fosters cultural understanding.

3. Mongolian Hospitality: Nomads are known for their warm hospitality. Engage in conversations, learn about their customs, and share stories around the campfire for a deeper connection.

4. Festivals and Celebrations: Plan your visit around local festivals, like Naadam, to witness traditional Mongolian sports and celebrations. These events offer a vibrant window into the culture.

Essential Tips:
1. Horse Riding Experience: While prior horseback riding experience is beneficial, beginners can also enjoy guided horse treks. Choose routes suitable for your skill level.

2. Pack Smart: Pack for various weather conditions, including warm layers, rain gear, and appropriate footwear for riding. Sun protection is crucial due to Mongolia's high altitude.

3. Responsible Tourism: Respect local customs, ask for permission before taking photos, and follow the principles of sustainable and respectful tourism.

4. Local Guides: Enlist the expertise of local guides who can navigate the terrain, offer cultural insights, and facilitate meaningful interactions with nomadic families.

Conclusion:

Mongolia's blend of horseback riding and nomadic culture offers a profound and immersive adventure for travelers seeking an authentic experience. From traversing diverse landscapes on horseback to sharing the daily lives of nomadic families, you'll create memories that resonate with the heart of Mongolia's heritage. By embracing the experiences and tips outlined in this guide, you'll embark on a transformative journey that celebrates the outdoors and the enduring spirit of the nomadic way of life in 2023.

Traditional Festivals

Cultural Experiences

Mongolia is a land of rich cultural heritage and vibrant traditions. Here are some traditional festivals you can experience during your visit:

1. Naadam Festival: One of Mongolia's most famous festivals, Naadam celebrates the "Three Manly Games" of wrestling, horse racing, and archery. Held in July, it offers a unique glimpse into Mongolian sports and culture.

2. Tsagaan Sar: Known as the Lunar New Year, Tsagaan Sar marks the beginning of spring. Families come together to welcome the new year with feasting, gift-giving, and visiting relatives.

3. Eagle Festival: Taking place in various regions, this festival showcases the ancient art of eagle hunting. Kazakh eagle hunters and their majestic birds compete in events that demonstrate their bond and hunting skills.

4. Golden Eagle Festival: Held in the Bayan-Ölgii Province, this festival is a showcase of traditional Kazakh customs and eagle hunting. Visitors can witness eagle hunting competitions, traditional performances, and local crafts.

5. Ovoo Worship: While not a formal festival, Ovoo worship is an essential part of Mongolian culture. Ovoos are sacred rock cairns found throughout the country, and locals offer prayers and offerings to them for protection and luck.

6. Thousand Camel Festival: Celebrated in the Gobi Desert, this festival highlights the importance of camels in the region. Visitors can enjoy camel races, cultural performances, and experience the unique desert environment.

7. Amarbayasgalant Festival: Held at the Amarbayasgalant Monastery, this festival celebrates the anniversary of the monastery's founding. It features religious ceremonies, traditional dances, and cultural exhibitions.

8. Nomad Day: This modern festival aims to preserve and promote nomadic traditions. It includes activities like traditional games, horse riding, and demonstrations of traditional crafts.

9. Ice Festival: Held on the frozen Lake Khövsgöl, this winter festival features ice sculpting, traditional games, and performances. It's a great opportunity to experience Mongolia's winter wonderland.

10. Gobi Camel Festival: Celebrated in the South Gobi Province, this festival highlights the role of camels in Gobi Desert life. Events include camel racing, traditional music, and cultural displays.

When attending these festivals, it's important to be respectful of local customs and traditions. Remember to ask for permission before taking photographs of people and seek guidance from locals to fully understand the significance of each event. Enjoy your cultural journey through Mongolia's traditional festivals in 2023!

Ger Camp Stays

Immersive Ger Camp Stays in Mongolia:

When you visit Mongolia, a unique cultural experience awaits you in the form of Ger camp stays. The traditional dwelling of the nomadic people, known as "Ger" in Mongolian or "Yurt" in other cultures, serves as both a home and a symbol of the nomadic lifestyle. Staying in a Ger camp allows you to connect with the local way of life, appreciate the stunning landscapes, and immerse yourself in the heart of Mongolian culture.

What to Expect:

1. Authentic Accommodation: Ger camps are typically set up in picturesque locations, ranging from rolling steppe to serene lakeshores. The Gers themselves are circular, felt-lined tents with a central stove for warmth. Despite their rustic appearance, they offer comfort and authenticity.

2. Warm Hospitality: Mongolian nomads are known for their warm hospitality. During your Ger camp stay, you'll have the chance to interact with the local hosts, learning about their daily routines, traditions, and way of life.

3. Culinary Delights: You'll be treated to traditional Mongolian cuisine, often centered around dairy products, meat, and staple foods. Taste "buuz" (steamed dumplings), "khorkhog" (meat cooked with hot stones), and "aaruul" (dried curds), among other dishes.

4. Cultural Insights: Engage in activities that offer insights into nomadic life. You might learn how to milk a cow or goat, help with herding, or even try your hand at traditional crafts like making felt or horsehair ropes.

5. Stargazing: With minimal light pollution, the Ger camp locations are ideal for stargazing. Enjoy the breathtaking beauty of the Mongolian night sky while seated around a campfire.

6. Disconnect to Reconnect: Most Ger camps lack modern amenities like electricity and internet, allowing you to disconnect from the digital world and fully immerse yourself in the natural surroundings.

Tips for Ger Camp Stays:

1. **Pack Appropriately:** Mongolian weather can be unpredictable, so bring layers and warm clothing even in summer.

2. **Respect Local Customs:** Be mindful of local customs and traditions. Ask for permission before taking photos of people or their property.

3. **Environmental Consciousness:** Leave no trace behind. Respect the delicate ecosystems and minimize your impact on the environment.

4. **Learn Basic Phrases:** While many Mongolians in tourist areas may speak some English, learning a few basic phrases in Mongolian can go a long way in building connections.

5. **Openness to Adventure:** Ger camps are a unique experience, but they might differ from the

comforts of a hotel. Embrace the adventure and enjoy the authenticity.

Staying in a Ger camp allows you to delve deep into the soul of Mongolia, fostering a connection to the land and its people that is truly unforgettable. So, don't miss the chance to experience the nomadic lifestyle firsthand during your 2023 journey to Mongolia!

Mongolian Cuisine

Savoring Mongolian Cuisine:

When exploring Mongolia, one of the most delightful cultural experiences is indulging in its unique cuisine. Reflecting the nomadic lifestyle and the country's rugged landscapes, Mongolian dishes are hearty, flavorful, and often prepared using traditional methods. Here's what you need to know about Mongolian cuisine:

Staple Ingredients:

1. Meat: Due to the pastoral nature of Mongolian life, meat plays a central role in the diet. Beef, mutton, and horse meat are commonly consumed. It's often prepared in stews, soups, and grilled dishes.

2. Dairy Products: Dairy holds cultural significance. You'll find various forms of dairy like yogurt ("tarag"), dried curds ("aaruul"), and fermented mare's milk ("airag").

3. Grains: While not as prevalent as meat and dairy, grains like wheat, barley, and millet are used in dishes like soups and porridges.

Signature Dishes:

1. Buuz: These steamed dumplings are a Mongolian favorite. Filled with minced meat and spices, they're traditionally prepared in large quantities for festive occasions.

2. Khorkhog: This dish involves cooking meat and vegetables with hot stones. The stones are heated in a fire, placed with the ingredients in a container, and covered to allow slow cooking.

3. Bantan: A hearty soup made from boiled meat (often mutton), and noodles or rice. It's a comforting dish enjoyed during colder months.

4. Boodog: A unique preparation involving cooking an entire animal (usually goat) by placing heated stones inside its body cavity.

5. Khuushuur: These deep-fried pockets of dough are filled with minced meat and are similar to dumplings, offering a satisfying crunch.

6. Tsagaan Idee: Known as "white food," this dish involves presenting various dairy products like yogurt, cheese, and curds in an aesthetically pleasing manner.

Cultural Aspects:

1. Hospitality: Mongolians are known for their hospitality. When offered food, it's customary to accept and enjoy what's served.

2. Traditional Techniques: Many dishes are prepared using traditional methods, such as cooking over an open flame or in hot stone containers.

3. Sharing Meals: Mongolian meals are often communal affairs, where friends and family gather around a shared platter.

4. Tea Culture: Milk tea, known as "suutei tsai," is a staple. It's a mixture of tea, milk, salt, and sometimes butter.

Tips for Enjoying Mongolian Cuisine:

1. Embrace the Adventure: Be open to trying new flavors and culinary techniques that may be unfamiliar.

2. Respectful Dining: When eating with locals, observe their customs, like not sticking chopsticks vertically into a bowl and using your right hand for passing and receiving food.

3. Food Allergies: If you have dietary restrictions or allergies, communicate them clearly, as Mongolian cuisine might contain ingredients that are new to you.

4. Ask Questions: Don't hesitate to ask your hosts or servers about the dishes and their preparation. Locals often enjoy sharing their culinary traditions.

Mongolian cuisine is a delightful way to connect with the country's culture and history. From hearty stews to unique cooking methods, every dish tells a story of nomadic life and the importance of sustenance in Mongolia's rugged landscapes. Enjoy exploring the flavors and traditions during your 2023 visit!

Arts and Crafts

Exploring Mongolian Arts and Crafts:

Mongolia's rich cultural heritage is beautifully expressed through its traditional arts and crafts. From intricate handwoven textiles to ornate carvings, the country's artistic traditions reflect its nomadic history and natural surroundings.

Traditional Arts:

1. Thangka Painting: Thangka paintings are intricate and vibrant depictions of Buddhist deities and scenes. These traditional artworks are often used for meditation and religious purposes.

2. Felt Making: Felt holds great significance in Mongolian culture. Nomadic herders use felt for everything from clothing to the construction of Gers (yurts). Intricately designed felt rugs and wall hangings are commonly found in homes and museums.

3. Woodcarving: Skilled artisans create delicate wood carvings, often featuring motifs inspired by nature, animals, and Buddhist symbols. These carvings adorn furniture, temples, and other structures.

4. Embroidery: Mongolian embroidery is known for its intricate patterns and vibrant colors. It's used to embellish clothing, accessories, and decorative items.

Crafts and Souvenirs:

1. Cashmere and Wool Products: Mongolia is renowned for its high-quality cashmere and wool products. Look for scarves, sweaters, and blankets made from locally sourced materials.

2. Silver and Metalwork: Intricate silver jewelry and metalwork are crafted by skilled silversmiths, often featuring traditional designs and symbols.

3. Pottery and Ceramics: While not as common as other crafts, Mongolian pottery showcases the unique artistic expressions of the region. You can find pottery with both utilitarian and decorative purposes.

4. Traditional Instruments: Musical instruments like the "morin khuur" (horsehead fiddle) and various drums are not only musical tools but also works of art, often adorned with intricate carvings.

Cultural Significance:

1. Nomadic Lifestyle: Many crafts are deeply intertwined with the nomadic way of life. Felt, for instance, serves as insulation in Gers and clothing, while embroidery often reflects the surrounding nature.

2. Spiritual Symbolism: Traditional arts often incorporate symbols and patterns inspired by Buddhism and shamanism, reflecting the spiritual beliefs of the people.

3. Storytelling: Through their intricate designs and depictions, Mongolian crafts often tell stories of the land, history, and beliefs, allowing you to connect with the culture on a deeper level.

Engaging with Arts and Crafts:

1. Workshops and Studios: Seek out workshops and studios where local artisans create and teach their crafts. Participating in a workshop can provide hands-on experience and insights into the creative process.

2. Markets and Souvenir Shops: Local markets and shops are great places to find authentic crafts. Engage with the artisans, ask questions, and learn about the stories behind their creations.

3. Ethnic Festivals: Many traditional festivals feature arts and crafts exhibitions. These events offer an opportunity to witness the diversity and creativity of Mongolian artisans.

4. Respect for Craftsmanship: When purchasing or viewing crafts, show respect for the skill and effort that goes into creating them. Ask about the materials used and the inspiration behind the piece.

Mongolia's arts and crafts are a testament to its cultural heritage and offer a window into the lives and beliefs of its people. Exploring these artistic traditions will undoubtedly enhance your understanding and appreciation of the country during your 2023 visit.

Historical Sites

Erdene Zuu Monastery

Certainly! In 2023, when visiting Mongolia, one of the remarkable historical sites to explore was the Erdene Zuu Monastery. Located in Kharkhorin (formerly Karakorum), this site holds immense historical significance as it is one of the oldest and most important monasteries in Mongolia.

Erdene Zuu Monastery was established in 1585 by Abtai Khan, a descendant of Genghis Khan, and it played a crucial role in the development of Buddhism in Mongolia. The monastery was built on the ruins of the ancient Mongol capital, Karakorum, and it served as both a religious center and a fortress. The construction style blends traditional Mongolian, Chinese, and Tibetan architectural elements.

Visitors to Erdene Zuu Monastery can explore its impressive walls, which consist of over 100 stupas, each containing sacred relics and artifacts. The central temple, Zuu of Buddha, is a focal point within the complex, housing statues, thangkas (Buddhist paintings), and other religious items. The monastery's museums provide insights into Mongolian history and culture, showcasing artifacts related to Buddhism and the region's heritage.

Exploring Erdene Zuu Monastery offers a glimpse into Mongolia's rich spiritual and cultural history, making it a must-visit destination for those interested in immersing themselves in the country's past. Additionally, the surrounding landscapes and the historic significance of the site add to the overall experience, providing visitors with a unique blend of history, architecture, and spirituality.

Ancient Petroglyphs

Certainly! In 2023, if you're interested in delving into Mongolia's historical treasures, exploring its ancient petroglyphs is a must-do activity. These captivating rock carvings offer a fascinating glimpse into the lives and cultures of Mongolia's past inhabitants.

The ancient petroglyphs, also known as rock engravings, are scattered across various regions of Mongolia. These intricate carvings on stone surfaces depict scenes from daily life, as well as animals, mythical creatures, hunting scenes, and symbols. These carvings were created by different cultures over thousands of years, contributing to the rich tapestry of Mongolia's history.

The locations of these petroglyphs are often chosen strategically, near water sources or in areas with historical significance. These sites not only showcase the artistic skills of ancient inhabitants but also provide insights into their spiritual beliefs, lifestyle, and interactions with their environment.

Some notable locations where you can find these ancient petroglyphs include the Tsagaan Salaa area, the Del Mountain area, and the Ikh Bogd Mountain range. These sites require some travel and exploration, adding to the adventure of discovering these historical treasures.

Visiting the ancient petroglyphs in Mongolia offers a unique opportunity to connect with the distant past and appreciate the artistry and stories left behind by ancient civilizations. It's a chance to step back in time and gain a deeper understanding of the cultures that have shaped Mongolia's history.

Karakorum and Genghis Khan's Legacy

Absolutely! When exploring Mongolia in 2023, a must-visit historical site is Karakorum, the ancient capital of the Mongol Empire, and the legacy of its legendary leader, Genghis Khan. This site offers a remarkable journey into Mongolia's past and the impact of one of history's most significant figures.

Karakorum, once a thriving city founded by Genghis Khan in the 13th century, served as the political, economic, and cultural center of the Mongol Empire. While much of the city's physical structures have been lost over time, the remnants and ruins that remain still carry a profound historical significance.

At the heart of Karakorum lies the Erdene Zuu Monastery, which I previously mentioned, a symbol of Genghis Khan's spiritual beliefs and a testament to the fusion of Mongolian, Chinese, and Tibetan cultural influences. The nearby Phallic

Rock, an ancient symbol of fertility, is another intriguing landmark in the area.

Exploring Karakorum today allows travelers to connect with Mongolia's imperial history and immerse themselves in the legacy of Genghis Khan. While the city itself might not be fully intact, the significance of the site is palpable, especially when considering its role in shaping the Mongol Empire and its influence on global history.

From learning about the military prowess and leadership of Genghis Khan to understanding the cultural exchanges that took place in the city, visiting Karakorum provides a comprehensive glimpse into the past, offering a profound appreciation for Mongolia's historical and cultural identity.

Wildlife and Nature

Endangered Species Conservation

Introduction:

Mongolia, a land of vast landscapes and untamed beauty, is a paradise for nature enthusiasts and wildlife lovers alike. In this travel guide, we will delve into the captivating world of Mongolia's wildlife and nature, highlighting its unique ecosystems, endangered species, and the efforts being made to conserve them.

1. Breathtaking Landscapes and Ecosystems:

Mongolia's diverse geography ranges from arid deserts to lush grasslands, rugged mountains, and pristine lakes. Explore the iconic Gobi Desert, witness the stunning Altai Mountains, and marvel at the serene waters of Khuvsgul Lake. These landscapes house a variety of ecosystems, each with its own unique flora and fauna.

2. Iconic Wildlife:

Mongolia is home to an array of captivating wildlife, from elusive snow leopards to the iconic wild horses known as Przewalski's horses. Other notable species include Siberian ibex, argali sheep, and various species of vultures and eagles. The Gobi Desert hosts the charming jerboa and the elusive Gobi bear.

3. Endangered Species Conservation:
As of 2023, Mongolia faces challenges in conserving its unique biodiversity due to factors like habitat loss, climate change, and illegal poaching. Efforts are being made by local and international organizations to protect and preserve these endangered species.

4. Snow Leopard Conservation:
The elusive snow leopard, a flagship species for Mongolia, is a top priority for conservation. Organizations like the Snow Leopard Trust collaborate with local communities to promote coexistence and reduce human-wildlife conflicts. Tracking and monitoring projects provide valuable insights into their behavior and movement patterns.

5. Przewalski's Horse Recovery:

The Przewalski's horse, once extinct in the wild, has seen successful reintroduction efforts. Conservationists work to ensure the survival of this species by reintroducing them to their natural habitat and implementing protective measures against predators and habitat degradation.

6. Protected Areas and National Parks:

Mongolia has established an extensive network of protected areas and national parks to safeguard its diverse ecosystems and wildlife. The Great Gobi Strictly Protected Area and the Hustai National Park are notable examples where visitors can witness conservation efforts firsthand.

7. Responsible Tourism and Eco-Friendly Practices:

Tourism in Mongolia has the potential to support conservation efforts. Responsible tourism practices, such as minimizing waste, respecting local customs, and adhering to ethical wildlife viewing guidelines, play a crucial role in maintaining the delicate balance between human activity and nature preservation.

Conclusion:

Mongolia's wildlife, nature, and endangered species conservation efforts offer a unique and enriching travel experience for adventurers and nature enthusiasts. By exploring its diverse landscapes and supporting responsible tourism, visitors contribute to the ongoing efforts to protect and preserve Mongolia's natural treasures for generations to come.

Bird Watching

Introduction:

Mongolia, a hidden gem for bird watchers, offers a captivating blend of untouched wilderness and diverse avian species. In this travel guide, we will explore the exciting world of bird watching in Mongolia, from its unique habitats to its stunning array of bird species.

1. Diverse Bird Habitats:

Mongolia's vast landscapes encompass a wide range of habitats, each providing a home to various bird species. From lush wetlands to high-altitude mountains and steppe grasslands, these habitats host a rich diversity of birdlife.

2. Avian Diversity:

Mongolia is a haven for bird enthusiasts, boasting over 450 species of birds. Endangered and rare species like the Saker Falcon, Eastern Imperial Eagle, and Pallas's Fish Eagle call this land home. You'll also find a variety of larks, warblers, cranes, and waterfowl.

3. Notable Birding Hotspots:

- Khustai National Park: Home to the endangered Great Bustard and other grassland species.
- Khuvsgul Lake: A paradise for waterfowl including swans, ducks, and gulls.
- Gorkhi-Terelj National Park: Explore mixed forests and spot woodpeckers, cuckoos, and flycatchers.
- Lake Buir: An important stopover for migratory birds on the East Asian-Australasian Flyway.

4. Migratory Routes:

Mongolia lies along the migratory routes of many bird species, making it a prime destination for witnessing incredible migrations. Every spring and autumn, flocks of birds traverse these landscapes, providing unforgettable sights for bird watchers.

5. Unique Species:

The critically endangered Oriental White Stork is a highlight for birders seeking rare sightings. Mongolia's diverse landscapes also offer a chance to spot the elusive Altai Snowcock, the striking Wallcreeper, and various species of eagles and falcons.

6. Local Birding Guides:

Local guides with deep knowledge of Mongolia's birdlife can enhance your bird watching experience. Their expertise and understanding of the terrain can lead you to the best spots for optimal bird sightings.

7. Responsible Bird Watching:

Respecting bird habitats and adhering to ethical guidelines is crucial. Avoid disturbing nesting sites, minimize noise, and maintain a respectful distance from the birds to ensure their safety and well-being.

Conclusion:

Mongolia's pristine landscapes and remarkable avian diversity make it an ideal destination for bird watchers seeking unique and breathtaking experiences. From rare and endangered species to stunning migrations, the country's natural beauty provides an unforgettable backdrop for birding adventures.

Flora and Fauna

Introduction:

Mongolia's untamed landscapes are a treasure trove of diverse flora and fauna, making it a haven for nature enthusiasts. In this travel guide, we'll delve into the captivating world of Mongolia's flora and fauna, highlighting its unique ecosystems and the remarkable species that call it home.

1. Biodiversity and Ecosystems:

Mongolia's geography spans deserts, mountains, grasslands, and lakes, resulting in a rich tapestry of ecosystems. These diverse habitats house a wide array of plant and animal species, adapted to thrive in extreme climates.

2. Indigenous Flora:

The flora of Mongolia is well-adapted to its arid climate. Vast steppes showcase resilient grasses like feather grass and fescue. In more sheltered areas, you'll find wildflowers like edelweiss and Siberian irises. Juniper forests and birch groves dot the landscape, adding to its botanical diversity.

3. Iconic Fauna:

Mongolia's wildlife is equally impressive, with species that have evolved to endure harsh conditions. The iconic Przewalski's horse, takhi, roams the grasslands. Snow leopards and elusive Gobi bears inhabit the remote corners of the country, while argali sheep and ibex thrive in mountainous regions.

4. Birdlife:

Mongolia is a paradise for bird enthusiasts, boasting over 450 bird species. Raptors like eagles and falcons soar in the skies, while wetlands support various waterfowl species, including cranes and swans. The country's varied habitats make it a crucial stopover for migratory birds.

5. Conservation Efforts:

Mongolia places a strong emphasis on conservation, recognizing the importance of preserving its unique flora and fauna. Protected areas like Gobi Gurvansaikhan National Park and Hustai National Park serve as crucial sanctuaries for endangered species and delicate ecosystems.

6. Wildlife Tracking and Research:

Numerous organizations collaborate with local communities to monitor and protect Mongolia's wildlife. Snow leopard tracking projects, for instance, provide valuable insights into the behavior and movement patterns of these elusive predators.

7. Responsible Nature Exploration:

Exploring Mongolia's wilderness comes with a responsibility to minimize impact. Adhering to Leave No Trace principles, respecting wildlife and their habitats, and traveling with eco-friendly practices in mind ensure the preservation of these delicate environments.

Conclusion:

Mongolia's remarkable flora and fauna offer a unique opportunity to immerse yourself in the beauty of untouched nature. From the resilient plant life to the captivating array of wildlife, every aspect of Mongolia's natural world tells a story of adaptation and survival. By exploring responsibly, visitors contribute to the ongoing preservation of these pristine landscapes for future generations to appreciate and cherish.

Practical Tips

Language and Communication

Language and Communication:

Mongolia's official language is Mongolian, which uses the Cyrillic script. However, English is becoming more widely spoken, especially in urban areas and among the younger population. In tourist hotspots, you're likely to find individuals who can communicate in basic English, making it easier for travelers to get around and find information.

Here are some practical tips for language and communication during your visit to Mongolia in 2023:

1. Learn Some Basic Phrases: While English is useful, learning a few essential Mongolian phrases can go a long way in showing respect for the local culture and engaging with locals. Simple greetings, thank you, and basic questions will be appreciated.

2. Translation Apps: Consider downloading translation apps on your smartphone. These can help bridge the language barrier by providing quick translations of text and spoken words. Apps like Google Translate can be a handy tool.

3. Guides and Interpreters: If you're planning to venture into more remote areas or wish to dive deeper into the local culture, hiring a local guide or interpreter can be incredibly valuable. They can help facilitate meaningful interactions and enhance your overall experience.

4. Bilingual Signage: In major cities and tourist areas, you'll often find signs and directions in both Mongolian and English. This makes navigating urban environments relatively straightforward.

5. Written Information: Tourist brochures, maps, and other informational materials are commonly available in English at hotels, visitor centers, and popular attractions. Make sure to grab these resources to aid in your exploration.

6. Body Language and Gestures: Sometimes, a smile or a nod can convey more than words. Being attentive to body language and nonverbal cues can help you navigate social situations with ease.

7. Local Etiquette: Mongolians are known for their hospitality and warmth. Politeness is highly regarded, so remember to say "sain bain uu" (hello) and "bayarlalaa" (thank you) as a sign of respect when interacting with locals.

8. Patience and Understanding: While communication might not always be seamless, approaching interactions with patience and a positive attitude can help you forge connections and overcome any language barriers.

In 2023, while English is becoming more prevalent, having a few language tools and strategies at your disposal can enhance your travel experience and enable you to connect more authentically with the people and culture of Mongolia.

Local Etiquette and Customs

Local Etiquette and Customs:

When traveling to Mongolia in 2023, it's important to be mindful of the local customs and etiquette to ensure a respectful and enjoyable experience. Mongolians take pride in their culture and traditions, and showing consideration for these practices will help you connect with locals on a deeper level.

Here are some practical tips for understanding and respecting local etiquette and customs:

1. Greetings: A traditional Mongolian greeting involves extending your right hand and offering a slight bow. While handshakes are becoming more common, especially in urban areas, it's still a good idea to be aware of the local greeting style.

2. Shoes and Entry: When entering someone's home, a temple, or a ger (traditional dwelling), it's customary to remove your shoes before stepping inside. This practice shows respect for the sacredness of the space.

3. Food and Drink: When invited to a meal, it's polite to try a little bit of everything that is offered. Accepting second helpings is often a sign of appreciation for the food. Remember to finish what's on your plate, as leaving food behind may be seen as wasteful.

4. Gift-Giving: Bringing a small gift when visiting someone's home is a thoughtful gesture. It doesn't have to be extravagant; something representative of your culture or a practical item is usually appreciated.

5. Respecting Elders: Mongolian society places a high value on respecting and honoring elders. If you're offered something by an older person, accept it with both hands as a sign of respect.

6. Dress Modestly: When visiting religious sites or rural areas, it's advisable to dress modestly, covering your shoulders and knees. This shows respect for local customs and traditions.

7. Photography: Always ask for permission before taking photos of people, especially in rural or nomadic settings. Many Mongolians are private individuals and may prefer not to be photographed.

8. Handling Money: When giving or receiving money, do so with your right hand, as the left hand is considered less clean. This applies to other objects and items as well.

9. Personal Space: While Mongolians are generally warm and friendly, they tend to maintain a bit more personal space during interactions compared to some Western cultures. Respect this by maintaining a comfortable distance.

10. Nomadic Culture: If you have the opportunity to visit nomadic families, be aware of their way of life. Gers are considered sacred spaces, and it's customary to walk clockwise when entering one.

By embracing these local customs and etiquette, you'll not only show respect for Mongolian traditions but also create meaningful connections with the people you meet. Remember that a genuine interest in the local culture will be warmly received and will enrich your travel experience in Mongolia in 2023.

Health and Safety

Health and Safety:

When traveling to Mongolia in 2023, ensuring your health and safety should be a top priority. While Mongolia offers unique landscapes and cultural experiences, it's important to be well-prepared and informed to have a safe and enjoyable trip.

Here are some practical tips for maintaining health and safety during your visit to Mongolia:

1. Travel Insurance: Before traveling, make sure you have comprehensive travel insurance that covers medical expenses, emergency evacuation, and other unforeseen situations. Check if your insurance also covers outdoor activities and adventure sports if you plan to engage in them.

2. Vaccinations: Consult your healthcare provider or a travel clinic well in advance to determine which vaccinations are recommended or required for Mongolia. Common vaccinations include those for hepatitis A, typhoid, and tetanus.

3. Medications and Prescriptions: Bring an ample supply of any prescription medications you require, along with a copy of your prescription. Ensure you have medications for common travel ailments such as diarrhea, allergies, and pain relief.

4. Altitude Sickness: If you plan to visit areas at higher altitudes, such as the Gobi Desert or certain mountainous regions, be aware of the risk of altitude sickness. Stay hydrated, avoid alcohol, and ascend gradually to allow your body to acclimatize.

5. Food and Water Safety: Stick to bottled water for drinking and brushing your teeth, and avoid consuming tap water or ice cubes. When dining, choose well-cooked and freshly prepared food to reduce the risk of foodborne illnesses.

6. Sun Protection: Mongolia's high elevation and open landscapes expose you to intense sunlight. Pack and use sunscreen, sunglasses, and a wide-brimmed hat to protect yourself from sunburn.

7. Insect Protection: In rural areas, especially during the warmer months, protect yourself from insect bites by wearing long sleeves and pants and using insect repellent.

8. Local Medical Facilities: In urban areas like Ulaanbaatar, medical facilities are available, but healthcare quality may vary. For serious medical issues, consider seeking care in larger cities or international clinics.

9. Emergency Contact Information: Save the contact information of your country's embassy or consulate in Mongolia, as well as local emergency numbers. Share your travel itinerary with a friend or family member for added safety.

10. Weather Preparedness: Mongolia's weather can be extreme, with temperature fluctuations between day and night. Pack appropriate clothing to stay warm, especially if you're traveling during colder months.

11. Wildlife Awareness: If you plan to explore the countryside, be cautious around wildlife. Avoid getting too close to animals, as some can be potentially dangerous.

12. Local Laws and Customs: Familiarize yourself with local laws and customs to avoid unintentional violations. Be respectful of cultural sensitivities, especially in religious or sacred sites.

By staying informed, taking necessary precautions, and being mindful of your health and safety, you can make the most of your journey through Mongolia and create lasting memories in 2023.

Sustainability and Responsible Travel

Eco-friendly Practices

Sustainability and Responsible Travel:
Eco-friendly Practices:

As you embark on your journey through Mongolia in 2023, embracing eco-friendly practices is essential to ensure the preservation of its pristine landscapes and unique ecosystems. Responsible travel not only benefits the environment but also supports local communities and promotes the long-term sustainability of the region.

Here are some eco-friendly practices to consider during your travels in Mongolia:

1. Respect Nature: Treat Mongolia's diverse landscapes, from the vast steppes to the rugged mountains, with care and respect. Stay on designated trails and paths to minimize soil erosion and protect delicate ecosystems.

2. Minimize Waste: Reduce your plastic waste by carrying a reusable water bottle, utensils, and cloth bags for shopping. Dispose of waste properly, using recycling facilities where available.

3. Choose Sustainable Accommodation: Opt for eco-friendly accommodations that prioritize energy efficiency, waste reduction, and responsible water use. Consider staying in traditional ger camps to support local communities.

4. Conserve Water: Water is a precious resource in Mongolia. Use water sparingly, especially in more remote areas where water availability may be limited.

5. Support Local Economy: Purchase locally made souvenirs, handicrafts, and products to contribute to the livelihoods of local artisans and reduce carbon emissions associated with importing goods.

6. Responsible Wildlife Viewing: When observing wildlife, maintain a respectful distance and avoid disturbing animals or their habitats. Refrain from feeding or approaching wild animals.

7. Cultural Sensitivity: Respect the traditions, customs, and way of life of the local people. Ask for permission before taking photos of individuals, and be mindful of your behavior in sacred or culturally sensitive areas.

8. Reduce Energy Consumption: Conserve energy by turning off lights, electronics, and heating when not in use. Choose accommodations that use renewable energy sources whenever possible.

9. Public Transportation and Shared Travel: When moving between destinations, consider using public transportation, shared vans, or group tours to reduce the carbon footprint of your travels.

10. Carbon Offsetting: If you're concerned about the environmental impact of your flights, consider carbon offsetting programs that allow you to invest in projects that reduce carbon emissions.

11. Participate in Conservation Efforts: Look for opportunities to engage in local conservation projects or community initiatives that focus on environmental protection and sustainability.

12. Leave No Trace: Leave the places you visit as you found them. Avoid leaving any litter or waste behind, and consider participating in organized clean-up activities if available.

By adopting these eco-friendly practices and embracing responsible travel, you can contribute to the preservation of Mongolia's stunning natural landscapes, support local communities, and make a positive impact on the environment in 2023 and beyond.

Supporting Local Communities

Sustainability and Responsible Travel: Supporting Local Communities:

When you travel to Mongolia in 2023, your choices as a responsible traveler can have a meaningful impact on local communities. Engaging in activities that directly support local residents can contribute to the social and economic well-being of the region, ensuring that your visit leaves a positive legacy.

Here are ways you can support local communities during your travels in Mongolia:

1. Stay in Locally-Owned Accommodations: Opt for guesthouses, ger camps, or lodges that are owned and operated by locals. Your accommodation expenses directly benefit the host community, providing employment and income.

2. Shop Locally: Purchase handicrafts, textiles, and souvenirs directly from local artisans and markets. This empowers local entrepreneurs and helps preserve traditional crafts.

3. Eat Local: Dine at local restaurants and food stalls to savor authentic Mongolian cuisine and contribute to the local economy. Try dishes prepared using locally sourced ingredients.

4. Participate in Community-Based Tourism: Engage in experiences that involve interaction with local communities, such as homestays or cultural workshops. This provides an opportunity to learn about traditional lifestyles while supporting livelihoods.

5. Respect Cultural Norms: When visiting nomadic families or remote villages, show respect for local customs and traditions. Seek permission before entering someone's home or taking photographs.

6. Employ Local Guides and Services: Hire local guides, drivers, and interpreters to enhance your experience and create direct employment opportunities within the community.

7. Contribute to Local Projects: Support community initiatives, schools, and conservation efforts through donations or participation. Look for opportunities to give back during your visit.

8. Learn and Interact: Engage with locals in a respectful and meaningful way. This could involve conversations, sharing experiences, and showing genuine interest in their lives.

9. Leave a Positive Impact: Minimize your impact on the environment and local resources. Dispose of waste properly, conserve water, and follow sustainable practices.

10. Responsible Souvenir Choices: Choose souvenirs that are ethically sourced and sustainable. Avoid products made from endangered species or materials that harm the environment.

11. Cultural Exchange: Share your own culture and experiences with locals, fostering a two-way exchange of ideas and fostering mutual understanding.

12. Feedback and Suggestions: Provide constructive feedback to accommodation providers and tour operators to help them improve their services and meet the needs of future travelers.

By supporting local communities through your travel choices, you can contribute to the well-being of the people you encounter and leave a positive mark on the places you visit. Responsible travel in Mongolia in 2023 means not only exploring the natural wonders but also engaging with the heart and soul of the region: its people.

Sample Itineraries

7 Days: Ulaanbaatar and Terelj

Day 1: Arrival in Ulaanbaatar

- Arrive in Ulaanbaatar, Mongolia's capital city.

- Check into your hotel and take some time to rest after your journey.

- Explore Sukhbaatar Square, the heart of the city, and visit the National Museum to learn about Mongolia's history.

Day 2: Ulaanbaatar City Tour

- Visit Gandan Monastery, one of Mongolia's most important Buddhist monasteries.

- Explore the Choijin Lama Temple Museum, showcasing religious artifacts and cultural heritage.

- Discover the Bogd Khan Winter Palace, a former residence of Mongolia's last king.

- Shop for souvenirs at the State Department Store or the Black Market.

Day 3: Terelj National Park

- Drive to Terelj National Park, about a 2-hour journey from Ulaanbaatar.
- Hike to the famous Turtle Rock and visit the Aryabal Meditation Temple.
- Experience nomadic culture by staying in a traditional ger (yurt) and enjoying local cuisine.

Day 4: Genghis Khan Statue Complex
- Enroute to Terelj, stop by the Genghis Khan Statue Complex, featuring a massive statue of the legendary leader.
- Learn about Genghis Khan's historical significance and enjoy panoramic views from the complex.

Day 5: Horseback Riding and Nature
- Enjoy a morning horseback ride through the picturesque landscapes of Terelj.
- Visit the Ovoo, a sacred stone heap, and learn about Mongolian shamanistic practices.
- Immerse yourself in the natural beauty of the park, taking leisurely walks or trying your hand at archery.

Day 6: Chinggis Khaan Square and Shopping

- Return to Ulaanbaatar.
- Stroll through Chinggis Khaan Square and visit the nearby Parliament House.
- Spend the afternoon shopping for cashmere products, traditional crafts, and local artwork.

Day 7: Departure
- Depending on your flight schedule, you may have some free time for last-minute exploration or relaxation.
- Check out from your hotel and proceed to the airport for your departure.

Please note that this is a sample itinerary and can be customized based on your preferences and travel dates. Make sure to check for any travel advisories or updates before your trip.

10 Days: Gobi Desert and Central Mongolia

Day 1: Arrival in Ulaanbaatar

- Arrive in Ulaanbaatar, Mongolia's capital city.

- Transfer to your hotel and settle in.

- Spend the evening exploring local markets and trying Mongolian cuisine.

Day 2: Ulaanbaatar City Tour

- Visit key attractions such as Gandan Monastery and the National Museum.

- Explore the vibrant Narantuul Market, also known as the "Black Market," for unique shopping experiences.

Day 3: South Gobi - Dalanzadgad

- Fly to Dalanzadgad, the gateway to the Gobi Desert.

- Explore Yolyn Am, a deep gorge with ice even in summer.

- Discover the unique flora and fauna of the Gobi region.

Day 4: Khongoryn Els Sand Dunes

- Drive to the Khongoryn Els sand dunes, known as the "Singing Dunes" due to the sound of the wind.
- Climb to the top for breathtaking desert views.
- Experience a camel ride across the dunes.

Day 5: Bayanzag (Flaming Cliffs)

- Visit Bayanzag, also known as the Flaming Cliffs, famous for dinosaur fossils.
- Explore the striking red rock formations and desert landscapes.

Day 6: Ongi Monastery Ruins

- Drive to the ruins of Ongi Monastery, a historic complex along the Ongi River.
- Learn about the history and culture of the area.

Day 7: Karakorum and Erdene Zuu Monastery

- Drive to Karakorum, the ancient capital of the Mongol Empire.
- Visit Erdene Zuu Monastery, one of the oldest and most important monastic complexes in Mongolia.

Day 8: Tsenkher Hot Springs

- Head to Tsenkher Hot Springs for a relaxing soak in natural thermal waters.
- Enjoy the scenic surroundings and rejuvenate after your journey.

Day 9: Terkhiin Tsagaan Lake (White Lake)
- Drive to Terkhiin Tsagaan Lake, located at the base of an extinct volcano.
- Explore the area's natural beauty and perhaps take a boat ride on the lake.

Day 10: Return to Ulaanbaatar and Departure
- Drive back to Ulaanbaatar.
- Spend your last evening shopping for souvenirs and enjoying a farewell dinner.
- Depart from Ulaanbaatar with unforgettable memories of your Mongolian adventure.

Remember that this is a suggested itinerary and can be adjusted to suit your interests and preferences. Check for any travel advisories or updates before your trip.

14 Days: Northern Adventure

Day 1: Arrival in Ulaanbaatar
- Arrive in Ulaanbaatar, Mongolia's capital city.
- Transfer to your hotel and get settled.
- Take an evening stroll through the city to get a taste of the local culture.

Day 2: Ulaanbaatar Exploration
- Explore Ulaanbaatar's historical sites, including Gandan Monastery and the National Museum.
- Visit Sukhbaatar Square and Parliament House.
- Dive into the city's bustling markets and try traditional Mongolian dishes.

Day 3: Terelj National Park
- Drive to Terelj National Park, known for its stunning landscapes.
- Visit Turtle Rock and hike to the Aryabal Meditation Temple.
- Experience nomadic culture by staying in a ger and participating in daily activities.

Day 4: Khustai National Park

- Journey to Khustai National Park, home to Przewalski's horse.
- Participate in wildlife observation and learn about conservation efforts.

Day 5-6: Amarbayasgalant Monastery
- Drive to Amarbayasgalant Monastery, a hidden gem of Mongolian architecture.
- Explore the serene surroundings and immerse yourself in the monastic culture.

Day 7-8: Khuvsgul Lake
- Travel to Khuvsgul Lake, often referred to as the "Blue Pearl of Mongolia."
- Enjoy boating, fishing, and hiking in the pristine wilderness.

Day 9-10: Reindeer Herders and Tsaatan Community
- Venture into remote regions to meet the Tsaatan community, known for their unique reindeer-herding lifestyle.
- Learn about their traditions and spend time with these remarkable people.

Day 11-12: Ulaan-Uul and Ulgii

- Drive to Ulaan-Uul and Ulgii in western Mongolia.
- Experience Kazakh culture, attend local festivals, and witness traditional eagle hunting.

Day 13: Return to Ulaanbaatar

- Fly back to Ulaanbaatar from Ulgii.
- Spend your last evening shopping for souvenirs and reminiscing about your journey.

Day 14: Departure

- Depending on your flight schedule, you might have some free time to explore or relax.
- Depart from Ulaanbaatar, carrying unforgettable memories of your northern Mongolian adventure.

Remember, this is a general guide and can be customized to suit your interests and travel dates. Always check for travel advisories and updates before your trip to ensure a safe and enjoyable experience.

Useful Resources

Maps and Navigation Apps

Mongolia Travel Guide 2023: Useful Resources - Maps and Navigation Apps

Introduction:
Mongolia, with its vast landscapes, nomadic culture, and unique experiences, has become an increasingly popular destination for adventurous travelers. Navigating this expansive country can be both exciting and challenging. To make the most of your journey, it's essential to have reliable maps and navigation apps at your fingertips. In this guide, we'll explore some of the best resources to ensure a smooth and memorable trip to Mongolia in 2023.

1. Google Maps:
Google Maps remains a top choice for travelers worldwide. It offers comprehensive maps, directions, and real-time traffic updates. Offline maps are particularly handy when you're exploring

remote areas with limited connectivity. Make sure to download the relevant maps before venturing into the less populated regions of Mongolia.

2. MAPS.ME:

MAPS.ME is a popular offline mapping app that allows you to download detailed maps of Mongolia before your trip. It features walking, cycling, and driving directions, along with points of interest. The offline mode ensures you can navigate even when you're off the grid.

3. OsmAnd:

OsmAnd is another excellent offline navigation app. It provides detailed, user-generated maps that are continually updated. Its unique feature is the ability to overlay GPX tracks, which is beneficial for trekkers and outdoor enthusiasts looking to explore Mongolia's stunning landscapes.

4. Here WeGo:

Here WeGo is known for its offline capabilities and provides detailed maps for Mongolia. The app offers public transportation information, real-time traffic data, and even bike routes. You can save your favorite places and routes for easy access throughout your journey.

5. MongolMap:
Specifically tailored for Mongolia, the MongolMap app is an excellent resource for travelers. It includes detailed maps, information about tourist attractions, and even some cultural insights. It's available offline, making it a valuable tool for your exploration.

6. Ulzi:
For safety-conscious travelers, Ulzi is an app that provides real-time tracking and emergency assistance. It's particularly useful if you're planning outdoor activities or heading to remote areas where communication might be limited.

7. Local Guides and Tour Operators:
While digital navigation tools are essential, don't underestimate the value of local knowledge. Engaging with local guides and tour operators can enhance your experience. They can provide

insights, suggest hidden gems, and offer guidance that goes beyond what navigation apps can offer.

Conclusion:

Navigating Mongolia's vast landscapes requires reliable maps and navigation apps that can handle both urban and rural environments. Whether you're exploring the capital city of Ulaanbaatar, embarking on a trek through the Gobi Desert, or visiting the iconic Mongolian steppe, having the right tools at your disposal will help you make the most of your journey. Combine digital resources with local expertise for an unforgettable travel experience in Mongolia in 2023.

Recommended Reading

Mongolia Travel Guide 2023: Useful Resources - Recommended Reading

Introduction:
Preparing for a trip to Mongolia goes beyond just planning the logistics. Immerse yourself in the country's rich history, culture, and landscapes by delving into some recommended reading before your journey. These books will provide you with valuable insights and enhance your overall travel experience in Mongolia in 2023.

1. "Genghis Khan and the Making of the Modern World" by Jack Weatherford:
This captivating book offers a deep dive into the life and legacy of Genghis Khan, the founder of the Mongol Empire. It sheds light on the historical and cultural context of Mongolia, providing an understanding of the country's past and its influence on the present.

2. "The Secret History of the Mongol Queens" by Jack Weatherford:

Continuing the narrative from his previous book, Weatherford explores the roles and impact of Mongol women throughout history. This book highlights the often-overlooked contributions of powerful women who shaped Mongolia's history and culture.

3. "Mongolia: Nomad Empire of the Eternal Blue Sky" by Carl Robinson:

For a comprehensive overview of Mongolia's geography, culture, and traditions, consider reading this book. It covers topics ranging from the country's nomadic lifestyle to its unique wildlife and stunning landscapes.

4. "The Blue Sky" by Galsan Tschinag:

Delve into the world of Mongolian nomadic culture through the eyes of Galsan Tschinag, a Tuvan writer. This novel offers a fictionalized account of a young boy's coming-of-age journey within the nomadic traditions of Mongolia.

5. "Three Cups of Tea: One Man's Mission to Promote Peace ... One School at a Time" by Greg Mortenson and David Oliver Relin:

While not exclusively about Mongolia, this book provides valuable insights into the challenges and rewards of development work in remote regions. It offers a different perspective on the impact of education and cultural exchange in countries like Mongolia.

6. "The Conqueror: A Novel of Kublai Khan" by Stephen R. Turnbull:

This historical novel brings to life the story of Kublai Khan, the grandson of Genghis Khan, who established the Yuan Dynasty in China. It offers a glimpse into the political intrigue and cultural interactions of the time.

7. "On the Trail of Genghis Khan: An Epic Journey Through the Land of the Nomads" by Tim Cope:

Join author Tim Cope on his remarkable journey as he retraces the route of Genghis Khan's cavalry across the vast steppes of Mongolia. This memoir provides a modern-day perspective on traveling through the country's remote regions.

Conclusion:

Reading about Mongolia's history, culture, and traditions before your trip can enrich your travel experience by providing context and depth to your explorations. Whether you're interested in historical figures, nomadic lifestyles, or modern-day adventures, these recommended books offer valuable insights into the country's past and present. Combine your reading with your physical journey for a truly immersive experience in Mongolia in 2023.

Online Travel Forums

Mongolia Travel Guide 2023: Useful Resources - Online Travel Forums

Introduction:
Planning a trip to Mongolia in 2023 involves more than just booking flights and accommodations. To make the most of your journey, tap into the wealth of knowledge and firsthand experiences shared by fellow travelers on online travel forums. These forums offer valuable insights, tips, and advice that can enhance your travel experience and help you navigate Mongolia with confidence.

1. TripAdvisor's Mongolia Forum:
TripAdvisor remains one of the most popular travel platforms, and its Mongolia Forum is a valuable resource for travelers seeking advice and information. Here, you can find discussions on topics ranging from itineraries and accommodations to transportation options and must-visit attractions. Don't hesitate to ask questions or contribute your own experiences.

2. Lonely Planet's Thorn Tree Forum:
Lonely Planet's Thorn Tree Forum is a long-standing community of travelers who share their insights and recommendations. In the Mongolia section, you'll find discussions about everything from visa requirements and safety tips to cultural etiquette and off-the-beaten-path destinations.

3. Reddit's r/Mongolia Subreddit:
Reddit is a versatile platform for discussions on various topics, and the r/Mongolia subreddit is a hub for discussions about the country. Here, you can connect with both travelers and locals to gain unique perspectives on travel, culture, and daily life in Mongolia.

4. Caravanistan Forum:
If you're planning an overland journey to Mongolia or through the Silk Road region, the Caravanistan Forum is a valuable resource. It's particularly useful for travelers embarking on road trips, border crossings, and long-distance adventures.

5. Expat and Traveler Blogs:

While not traditional forums, many expat and traveler blogs provide in-depth insights into life and travel in Mongolia. These personal accounts often contain practical tips, cultural observations, and firsthand experiences that can be highly beneficial for travelers.

6. Facebook Groups:
Facebook has numerous groups dedicated to travel in Mongolia. Look for groups like "Travel Mongolia" or "Mongolia Travel Community" where travelers share their stories, photos, and advice. These groups are also great for connecting with fellow travelers who might be planning similar itineraries.

7. Local Forums and Websites:
Exploring local Mongolian forums or travel websites can provide you with insights from residents and local experts. These sources can offer a unique perspective and up-to-date information on events, festivals, and hidden gems.

Conclusion:

Online travel forums offer an invaluable opportunity to tap into the collective wisdom of experienced travelers and enthusiastic locals. From practical travel advice to cultural insights, these forums provide a platform for sharing and learning that can greatly enhance your journey in Mongolia in 2023. Engage with the community, ask questions, and contribute your experiences to create a well-rounded and informed travel experience.

Conclusion

Mongolia Travel Guide 2023: Conclusion

Embrace the Adventure:

As your journey through Mongolia in 2023 comes to a close, you'll likely find yourself reflecting on the captivating landscapes, rich cultural experiences, and unforgettable moments that have defined your trip. From the vast expanses of the Gobi Desert to the rugged beauty of the Altai Mountains, Mongolia's diverse landscapes have a way of leaving a lasting imprint on travelers.

Nomadic Traditions and Warm Hospitality:

Immersing yourself in Mongolia's nomadic traditions offers a unique opportunity to connect with a way of life that has endured for centuries. The warm hospitality of the Mongolian people welcomes you into their ger camps, offering a glimpse into their daily routines, traditional practices, and genuine camaraderie.

Respect for Nature and Culture:

As you've traversed the country, you've likely come to appreciate the profound respect that Mongolians have for their natural surroundings and cultural heritage. The interconnectedness between the land and the people is evident in the way traditions are upheld, and the environment is cherished. Your role as a responsible traveler involves preserving this delicate balance by minimizing your impact and embracing sustainable practices.

An Unforgettable Tapestry:
Mongolia is a place where ancient history, modern aspirations, and untouched wilderness converge to create an unforgettable tapestry of experiences. From the majestic ruins of Karakorum to the bustling markets of Ulaanbaatar, you've encountered a spectrum of moments that paint a vivid picture of the country's complex identity.

Continued Exploration:
As your journey draws to a close, remember that Mongolia's allure is boundless. Whether you're drawn back by the call of the steppes, the intrigue of cultural festivals, or the promise of new

adventures, this vast land will always welcome you with open arms.

Beyond Borders:

Your experience in Mongolia goes beyond the physical borders you've explored. It encompasses the stories you've shared, the connections you've made, and the understanding you've gained. Carry these memories and insights with you, and let them continue to inspire your journey, both within and beyond Mongolia's horizons.

Until We Meet Again:

As you bid farewell to Mongolia, remember that your journey isn't ending; it's simply transitioning into the next chapter. Let the spirit of Mongolia's landscapes and people accompany you on your future travels and endeavors, and know that the memories you've created here will remain a cherished part of your personal tapestry.

Safe travels, and may your adventures continue to unfold with the same sense of wonder that Mongolia has awakened within you.

THANK YOU

Dear valued customers, if you enjoyed using our travel guides, we would be grateful if you could take just 5 seconds to leave a review.

Your feedback is highly appreciated and will help others make informed decisions about our products.

Thank you for choosing our travel guides and for your continued support!

Printed in Great Britain
by Amazon